Writer's Choice
Grammar and Composition

Vocabulary and Spelling Strategies and Practice

Grade 6

Glencoe McGraw-Hill

New York, New York   Columbus, Ohio   Woodland Hills, California   Peoria, Illinois

Glencoe/McGraw-Hill

A Division of The McGraw·Hill Companies

Copyright © The McGraw-Hill Companies, Inc. All rights reserved. Permission is granted to reproduce material contained herein on the condition that such material be reproduced only for classroom use; and be provided to students, teachers, and families without charge; and be used solely in conjunction with *Writer's Choice*. Any other reproduction, for use or sale, is prohibited without written permission of the publisher.

Printed in the United States of America.

Send all inquiries to:
Glencoe/McGraw-Hill
8787 Orion Place
Columbus, Ohio 43240

ISBN 0-07-823251-1

1 2 3 4 5 6 7 8 9   045   04 03 02 01 00

Contents

Case Study Vocabulary

    Pinkney Records a Round-the-World Voyage 1
    Katz Rides the *Empire Builder* 2
    Boulanger Describes Nunataks 3
    Hamilton Narrates a Life 4
    Tribune Explores Hang Time 5
    Anderson Fights for the Planet 6

Literature Vocabulary

    The Invisible Thread, by Yoshiko Uchida 7
    Coast to Coast, by Betsy Byars 8
    Morning Girl, by Michael Dorris 9
    "The Jacket," by Gary Soto 10
    "Bathing Elephants," by Peggy Thomson 11
    "Thanking the Birds," by Joseph Bruchac 12

Learning from Context

    Definition I 13
    Definition II 14
    Example I 15
    Example II 16
    Comparison I 17
    Comparison II 18
    Contrast I 19
    Contrast II 20

Word Parts

    Roots I 21
    Roots II 22
    Prefixes I 23
    Prefixes II 24
    Prefixes III 25
    Suffixes I 26
    Suffixes II 27
    Suffixes III 28

Contents

Synonyms, Antonyms, and Homonyms

Synonyms I 29
Synonyms II 30
Antonyms I 31
Antonyms II 32
Homonyms 33
Borrowed Words 34

Using the Dictionary

Using the Dictionary I 35
Using the Dictionary II 36
Using the Dictionary III 37
Using the Dictionary IV 38
Using the Dictionary V 39
Using the Dictionary VI 40

Using Spelling Rules

Spelling *ie* and *ei* 41
Suffixes and the Silent *e* 42
Suffixes and the Final *y* 43
Doubling the Final Consonant 44
Forming Compound Words 45
General Rules for Forming Plurals 46
Special Rules for Forming Plurals I 47
Special Rules for Forming Plurals II 48

Troublesome Words

Troublesome Words I 49
Troublesome Words II 50
Troublesome Words III 51
Troublesome Words IV 52

Answers 53

Vocabulary and Spelling Strategies and Practice

Name .... Class .... Date ....

1 Pinkney Records a Round-the-World Voyage

Use with Writing in the Real World, pp. 4–7.

Key Information

The words listed below will help you understand Writing in the Real World. Say each word to yourself. Then answer the questions that follow.

sprint	navigation	longitude	visible
determination	glimpse	latitude	recall

■ A. Exploring Word Meanings

In the space provided, write your answer to each question. Use a dictionary if you need help.

1. Which word has the same meaning as *remember?*

   _____

2. If you were writing about whether you could see something, which two words might you use? _____

3. Which two words might you use to write about a runner who is trying with all her might to win the 100-yard dash? _____

4. Which three words could be grouped under the heading Sailing?

   _____

■ B. Using Words in Sentences

Write a definition of the underlined word based on its use in the sentence. Use a dictionary if you need help.

1. Jamal saw his friend <u>sprint</u> out the door as soon as school was over.

   _____

2. Until explorers learned about <u>navigation</u>, people rarely crossed the vast oceans.

   _____

3. The door closed so quickly that Molly could only <u>glimpse</u> what was going on behind it.

   _____

4. The tents of the mountain climbers were barely <u>visible</u> in the snowstorm.

   _____

5. The <u>latitude</u> of a point on the surface of the earth is measured north or south from the equator.

   _____

Writer's Choice: Vocabulary and Spelling Strategies and Practice, Grade 6   **1**

Vocabulary and Spelling Strategies and Practice

Name .... Class .... Date ....

2 | Katz Rides the *Empire Builder*

Use with Writing in the Real World, pp. 38–41.

> **Key Information**
>
> The words listed below will help you understand Writing in the Real World. Say each word to yourself. Then complete the exercises that follow.
>
> surrender   retreat   manuscript
> additional   resist   embellish

■ A. Exploring Word Meanings

Imagine you are a captain in a battle. Your troops are outnumbered. You must decide whether to surrender, resist, or retreat. Explain briefly what your troops might do in each case. Use a dictionary if you need help.

1. surrender _____
2. resist _____
3. retreat _____

■ B. Using Words in Sentences

Rewrite each sentence. Replace the underlined word or words with a word from the list above. You can check meanings in a dictionary.

1. In his telegram to the general the captain asked for <u>extra</u> troops.

   _____
   _____

2. The general decided to <u>decorate</u> his plain uniform with gold braid.

   _____
   _____

3. The <u>handwritten document</u> gave an eyewitness account of the battle.

   _____
   _____

4. Evelyn had to <u>fight against</u> the urge to get off the train and stay in the mountains.

   _____
   _____

5. The losing team would not <u>step back</u> from its position in the debate.

   _____
   _____

Vocabulary and Spelling Strategies and Practice

Name .... Class .... Date ....

3 Boulanger Describes Nunataks

Use with Writing in the Real World, pp. 102–105.

Key Information

The words listed below will help you understand Writing in the Real World. Say each word to yourself. Then complete the exercises that follow.

| glacier | vivid | boulder | scamper | isolated |
| expand | resemble | variety | wildlife | continuously |

■ A. Understanding Definitions

Read each definition below. Write the word from the list that matches each definition. Refer to a dictionary as needed.

1. animals, birds, and fishes in a natural area _____
2. look like _____
3. alone; separate _____
4. collection of different things _____
5. run quickly and playfully _____
6. large rounded rock _____
7. huge mass of ice moving over land _____
8. grow bigger _____
9. over and over again _____
10. colorful and lively _____

■ B. Using Words in Sentences

Answer each question in a complete sentence. In your answer use at least one vocabulary word from this lesson.

1. Could a boulder resemble an egg? _____

2. Is wildlife found in isolated areas? _____

3. Are snakes a variety of animal that can scamper? _____

Vocabulary and Spelling Strategies and Practice

Name .... Class .... Date ....

4 Hamilton Narrates a Life

Use with Writing in the Real World, pp. 144–147.

> **Key Information**
>
> The words listed below will help you understand Writing in the Real World. Say each word to yourself. Then answer the questions that follow.
>
> | protest | solemn | organize | honor |
> |---|---|---|---|
> | significance | rally | impress | courageous |

■ A. Using Words to Describe

Write two words from the list above that you might use in a paragraph about each of the following. Consult a dictionary if you need to be sure of each word's meaning.

1. an important occasion

2. a civil rights worker

■ B. Using Words in Sentences

Write a definition of each underlined word, based on its use in the sentence. Check meanings in a dictionary as needed.

1. Don't try to <u>impress</u> others with your knowledge.

2. Louise recognized the <u>significance</u> of her friend's achievement.

3. Many people <u>honor</u> the accomplishments of Martin Luther King Jr.

4. An activist might <u>organize</u> many people to march in a rally to show support for a law.

5. <u>Sophisticated</u> people are skilled at working directly with government leaders.

6. The <u>courageous</u> firefighters entered the burning building.

7. Glen's father joined in the <u>protest</u> against unfair labor practices.

8. At the <u>rally</u> a hundred people gathered to hear the mayor's speech.

4 Writer's Choice: *Vocabulary and Spelling Strategies and Practice,* Grade 6

Vocabulary and Spelling Strategies and Practice

Name .... Class .... Date ....

5 | *Tribune* Explores Hang Time

Use with Writing in the Real World, pp. 182–185.

> **Key Information**
> The words listed below will help you understand Writing in the Real World. Say each word to yourself. Then answer the questions that follow.
>
> | | | | |
> |---|---|---|---|
> | defy | explosive | technique | gravity |
> | feature | force | challenge | pose |

■ A. Forming Word Groups

Add a word from the list above to make a group of related words. Use a dictionary as needed.

1. camera, position, _____
2. bomb, noisy, _____
3. method, procedure, _____
4. power, strength, _____
5. resist, dare, _____
6. atmosphere, weight, _____
7. dare, task, _____

■ B. Understanding Word Meanings

Answer each question in a sentence, using a word from the list above. Use a dictionary as needed.

1. What might a person defy?
   _____

2. How might you pose a friend for a photograph?
   _____

3. What are some features of your face?
   _____

4. How might a construction worker use force?
   _____

5. Why do athletes imitate Jordan's technique?
   _____

6. What is the biggest challenge you have faced?
   _____

Writer's Choice: Vocabulary and Spelling Strategies and Practice, Grade 6   **5**

Vocabulary and Spelling Strategies and Practice

Name .... Class .... Date ....

6 Anderson Fights for the Planet

Use with Writing in the Real World, pp. 218–221.

> **Key Information**
>
> The words listed below will help you understand Writing in the Real World. Say each word to yourself. Then answer the questions that follow.
>
> | | | |
> |---|---|---|
> | pollution | conserve | segment |
> | accuracy | persuade | convey |

■ A. Understanding Words Through Examples

Each item gives two examples of possible meanings for a word listed above. Write that word in the first blank. Then add another example in the second blank. Use a dictionary as needed.

1. Word: _____
   Examples: a piece of an orange
   the part of a television show between two commercial breaks
   _____

2. Word: _____
   Examples: chemicals dumped into a stream
   acid rain
   _____

3. Word: _____
   Examples: to save food when camping so there is something to eat each day
   to protect a forest so people in the future can enjoy it
   _____

4. Word: _____
   Examples: to transport vegetables in a truck
   to carry a message to someone
   _____

5. Word: _____
   Examples: to talk a friend into seeing the movie of your choice
   to get your parents to agree to raise your allowance
   _____

■ B. Using Words in Sentences

Write a sentence using each word correctly. Use a dictionary as needed.

1. conserve _____
   _____

2. accuracy _____
   _____

Vocabulary and Spelling Strategies and Practice

Name .... Class .... Date ....

7 | *The Invisible Thread,* Yoshiko Uchida

Use with Unit 1, pp. 28–34.

Key Information

Listed below are some important words from the literature selection. Say each word to yourself.

immense	procedure	furiously
survey	amble	simultaneously

■ A. Linking Definitions and Parts of Speech

Match each definition with a word from the list above. Then write whether the word is used as a noun, verb, adjective, or adverb. Consult a dictionary as needed.

Definition	Word	Part of Speech
1. set of steps for doing a task		
2. extremely large		
3. look over the whole situation		
4. with anger or fierce excitement		
5. walk without hurrying		
6. at the same time		

■ B. Using Words in Sentences

Complete each sentence, using a word from the list above.

1. Aminah told her sister to hurry and not to _____, because the storm was fast approaching.

2. One _____ dark cloud was moving their way.

3. The storm raged _____ leaving behind broken branches and scattered trash cans.

4. Sherrie and Donna knew the correct _____ to follow if they heard a tornado warning.

5. When Donna took shelter in the house, she heard the telephone and the doorbell ringing _____.

6. After the storm the girls walked around the neighborhood to _____ the damage.

Vocabulary and Spelling Strategies and Practice

Name .... Class .... Date ....

8 | *Coast to Coast,* Betsy Byars

Use with Unit 2, pp. 82–87.

> **Key Information**
>
> The words listed below are important for understanding the literature selection. Read each word to yourself.
>
> | idle | throttle | hangar |
> |---|---|---|
> | altimeter | strut | taxiway |

■ A. Understanding Definitions

All the words in the list relate to airplanes. Write the word from the list that matches each definition. Check meanings in a dictionary as needed.

1. large shelter for an airplane _____
2. device for measuring altitude _____
3. paved strip used by airplanes when moving on the ground _____
4. to run an engine with gears disengaged _____
5. lever that controls the fuel supply _____
6. supporting bar between the body of the plane and the wing _____

■ B. Exploring Word Meanings

Write a brief answer to each question, using the vocabulary words from the lesson.

1. Why is an altimeter important to an airplane pilot?
   _____
   _____

2. Can an airplane idle while it is in a hangar? Explain.
   _____
   _____

3. If the strut under an airplane wing broke during flight, what might happen?
   _____
   _____

4. How do you think a taxiway is different from a runway?
   _____
   _____

Vocabulary and Spelling Strategies and Practice

Name .... Class .... Date ....

9 | *Morning Girl,* Michael Dorris

Use with Unit 3, pp. 134–140.

> **Key Information**
>
> The words listed below are important for understanding the literature selection. Say each word on the list to yourself.
>
> | patience | curious | memorized | complicated |
> |---|---|---|---|
> | confessed | spiral | reflection | |

■ A. Forming Word Groups

Add a word from the list above to make a group of related words. Check a dictionary if you need help.

1. mirror, image, _____
2. admitted, told, _____
3. coil, circle, _____
4. calmness, tolerance, _____
5. difficult, complex, _____
6. learned, recalled, _____
7. questioning, interested, _____

■ B. Clarifying Meaning

Read each sentence. Then write another sentence to help explain the underlined word.

1. The test was very <u>complicated</u>. _____
_____

2. She planted flowers in the garden in the shape of a <u>spiral</u>. _____
_____

3. The class could tell that Roosevelt had <u>memorized</u> the poem. _____
_____

4. Brian showed <u>patience</u> while looking after the five puppies. _____
_____

5. Aviva stared at the floor for a moment and then <u>confessed</u>. _____
_____

6. The unusual shape of the leaf on the grass made the girls <u>curious</u>. _____
_____

Vocabulary and Spelling Strategies and Practice

Name .... Class .... Date ....

10 "The Jacket," Gary Soto

Use with Unit 4, pp. 172–178.

> **Key Information**
>
> Listed below are some useful words from the literature selection. Say each word on the list to yourself.
>
> | | | | |
> |---|---|---|---|
> | hurl | vinyl | embarrassed | vicious |
> | profile | terrorist | braille | camouflage |

■ A. Making Word Associations

Write a word from the list above that has a close connection with each of the following. Use each word once. Consult a dictionary as needed.

1. a soldier _____
2. a blind person _____
3. a javelin thrower _____
4. a car seat _____
5. a mean dog _____
6. a face on a coin _____
7. a bomb thrower _____
8. a shy person _____

■ B. Rewriting Sentences

Rewrite each sentence, using the word provided. Change the sentence as much as you want.

1. The hunters wore dull green and brown outfits to blend in with the woods. (camouflage)

   _____
   _____

2. The outline of the giant rock looked like a human face turned sideways. (profile)

   _____
   _____

3. Marie moved her fingers over the tiny raised dots on the page of her book. (braille)

   _____
   _____

4. Angelique threw the tennis ball over the fence with all her might. (hurled)

   _____
   _____

5. The dog became fierce and dangerous because its owners mistreated it. (vicious)

   _____
   _____

Vocabulary and Spelling Strategies and Practice

Name .... Class .... Date ....

11   "Bathing Elephants," Peggy Thomson

Use with Unit 5, pp. 210–214.

Key Information

Listed below are words that are important for understanding the literature selection. Read each word on the list to yourself.

wilt	infection	fissure	vulnerable
unsightly	maneuver	awe	vibrate

■ A. Recognizing Word Clues

Write the word from the list that best matches each description. Consult a dictionary as needed.

1. Lava might ooze out of this in a volcano. _____
2. Flowers do this from lack of water. _____
3. Animals and people suffer pain and illness as a result of this. _____
4. The walls of a house do this during a mild earthquake. _____
5. A very messy room could be described this way. _____
6. A cat without claws to defend itself is this. _____
7. People looking at fireworks in the sky might show this. _____

■ B. Using Words in Sentences

Write a sentence of your own, using each word given. Use a dictionary to make sure you have used the word correctly.

1. vulnerable _____
   _____

2. vibrate _____
   _____

3. wilt _____
   _____

4. unsightly _____
   _____

5. maneuver _____
   _____

6. infection _____
   _____

Writer's Choice: Vocabulary and Spelling Strategies and Practice, Grade 6   **11**

Vocabulary and Spelling Strategies and Practice

Name .... Class .... Date ....

12 "Thanking the Birds," Joseph Bruchac

Use with Unit 6, pp. 242–246.

> **Key Information**
>
> Listed below are some words from the literature selection. Read each word on the list to yourself.
>
> | | | | |
> |---|---|---|---|
> | lecture | continent | anecdote | ritual |
> | sacred | game | similarity | chickadee |

■ A. Forming Word Groups

Add a word from the list above to make a group of related words. Consult a dictionary if you need help.

1. speech, classroom, _____
2. robin, blue jay, _____
3. tradition, ceremony, _____
4. story, personal, _____
5. holy, respected, _____
6. birds, deer, hunting, _____
7. likeness, shared, _____
8. land, North America, _____

■ B. Linking Words to a Main Idea

Cross out the word in each group that does not belong with the other two. Then choose the correct main idea for each group of two and write it on the line.

    Main Ideas: animals   religion   communication

1. game, chickadee, sacred _____
2. ritual, sacred, game _____
3. lecture, ritual, anecdote _____

12 Writer's Choice: *Vocabulary and Spelling Strategies and Practice*, Grade 6

Vocabulary and Spelling Strategies and Practice

Name .... Class .... Date ....

13 Learning from Context: Definition I

Key Information

Suppose you are puzzled by a new word while reading. Often you can figure out the meaning from the context—the surrounding words and sentences. Sometimes, a definition of the word is given in the sentence that includes the word.

The rock was *pulverized;* that is, it was crushed into tiny bits.

The clue words *that is* tell you that the word *pulverized* means "crushed into tiny bits." Below are some clue words that can help you spot definitions in context.

that is   in other words   which means

■ A. Noticing Definitions

Use context clues to figure out the meaning of the underlined word in each sentence. Write the word and its meaning on the line.

1. The base of the telescope is <u>stationary</u>, which means it cannot be moved.
   _____

2. Maurice is <u>avid</u> about bird watching; in other words, he is enthusiastic about this hobby.
   _____

3. The cave was <u>musty</u>; that is, it smelled damp and moldy.
   _____

4. <u>Voles</u>, which are small, mouselike animals, dig tunnels in the ground.
   _____

5. The rabbit <u>eluded</u> the fox; that is, it escaped.
   _____

■ B. Using Context Clues in Sentences

Complete each sentence by defining the underlined word. Check the meaning of the word in a dictionary before you write.

1. Both camels and sheep are <u>ruminants</u>, which means that they _____
   _____

2. As Tina told her story, she began to <u>meander</u>; in other words, she _____
   _____

3. For Anthony's family, celebrating grandmother's birthday was a <u>tradition</u>; that is, they
   _____

Vocabulary and Spelling Strategies and Practice

Name .... Class .... Date ....

14 Learning from Context: Definition II

Key Information

The following sentence includes a definition that is introduced by a clue word.

How the dinosaurs became extinct remains an *enigma,* or mystery.

The clue word *or* tells you that the word *enigma* means "mystery." Below are some additional clue words that can help you spot definitions in context.

| or | which is called | also known as |

■ A. Noticing Definitions

Use clue words to figure out the meaning of the underlined word. Write the word and its meaning on the line.

1. Yelena is very shrewd, or clever, in solving number puzzles.

   _____

2. The study of minerals, which is called mineralogy, appeals to many people.

   _____

3. Dry creeks, also known as arroyos, run through this part of the desert.

   _____

4. Eliot burnished, or polished, the copper kettle until it was as shiny as a new penny.

   _____

5. The climbers carefully crossed a deep crack, or crevasse, in the glacier.

   _____

■ B. Using Context Clues in Sentences

Complete each sentence by giving the meaning of the underlined word. Be as specific as you can. Check meanings in a dictionary as needed.

1. A porcupine has quills, or _____ on its back.
2. The _____, which is called a flamingo, flew past Kuniko in the marsh.
3. Ernesto's favorite activity on weekends is _____, also known as hiking.

14 Writer's Choice: Vocabulary and Spelling Strategies and Practice, Grade 6

Vocabulary and Spelling Strategies and Practice

Name .... Class .... Date ....

15 Learning from Context: Example I

Key Information

Sometimes writers use familiar examples to help readers understand an unfamiliar word, as in this sentence.

   My uncle is very *frugal;* for example, he mends his old socks instead of buying new ones.

The words *for example* introduce an example of being frugal. From the example you can guess that *frugal* means "thrifty," or "unwilling to spend money needlessly." Writers often use the words below when giving examples.

   for example   such as

■ A. Noticing Examples

Each sentence below includes examples. Use the examples and the clue words to figure out the meaning of the underlined word. Write the word and a brief definition on the line.

1. The top of the box should be covered with a transparent material, such as glass or clear plastic.

   _____

2. My aunt pampers her prize-winning cat; for example, she feeds it expensive tuna and gives it a velvet pillow to sleep on.

   _____

3. Rodents, such as mice, hamsters, and rabbits, have sharp front teeth for gnawing.

   _____

4. The peasants' supper was always meager; for example, tonight each person had only a small potato and one slice of bread.

   _____

5. When asked about his project, William gave vague answers, such as "Maybe" or "I'll have to wait and see."

   _____

■ B. Using Context Clues in Sentences

Complete each sentence by adding examples that make clear the meaning of the underlined word. Check the word in a dictionary if you need help.

1. Dressed for the ball, the young woman looked regal; for example, she wore

   _____

2. The rooms of the old house were filled with antiques, such as _____

   _____

Writer's Choice: Vocabulary and Spelling Strategies and Practice, Grade 6   **15**

Vocabulary and Spelling Strategies and Practice

Name .... Class .... Date ....

16 Learning from Context: Example II

> **Key Information**
>
> In the following sentence, the writer includes examples to help the reader understand an unfamiliar word.
>
> A *shrill* noise, like that from a teakettle, came from the distant fishing boat.
>
> Notice that the clue word *like* introduces the example. From this example, you can guess that *shrill* means "high-pitched." Writers often use the words below when giving examples.
>
> like   including

■ A. Noticing Examples

Use the example or examples in each sentence to figure out the meaning of the underlined word. Write the word and a brief definition on the line. Then use a dictionary to check meanings.

1. Darcy's hair is <u>auburn</u>, like the color of cinnamon.
   _____

2. Hoofed animals, including elephants, horses, cattle, and deer, are <u>ungulates</u>.
   _____

3. Toronto is a <u>metropolis</u>, like Tokyo, New York, and Los Angeles.
   _____

4. Trees called <u>conifers</u>, including pines, firs, and spruces, are green all year round.
   _____

■ B. Using Examples to Clarify

Complete each sentence by adding words that help clarify the underlined word. Check meanings in a dictionary as needed.

1. Many <u>crustaceans</u>, including lobsters, shrimp, and crabs, _____
   _____

2. The control panel of an airplane has several <u>meters</u>, including _____
   _____

3. Rena named things that are <u>drab</u> in color, such as _____
   _____

Vocabulary and Spelling Strategies and Practice

Name .... Class .... Date ....

17 Learning from Context: Comparison I

> **Key Information**
>
> When you come across an unfamiliar word, look at the surrounding words and sentences. These make up the context. Often, the context contains clues to the word's meaning. In the following sentence, the unfamiliar word is compared to something familiar.
>
> Martinsburg is just a *hamlet;* similarly, Fredericktown is a small village.
>
> The word *similarly* introduces a comparison. The comparison helps you figure out that *hamlet* means "small village." Here are two words writers often use when making comparisons.
>
> similarly   as

■ A. Using Words in Sentences

Write a definition for the underlined word in each sentence. Check your definition in a dictionary.

1. The warmed block of wax was as <u>pliable</u> as putty.
2. Sam wore a <u>vacant</u> expression; Sean's face was similarly blank.
3. The bite of a rattlesnake is usually <u>lethal</u> to a mouse; similarly, the venom of the cobra is deadly to small animals.
4. Hiking on the trails, Ella's sixty-year-old uncle was as <u>nimble</u> as a mountain goat.

■ B. Inferring Meaning

Complete each sentence to clarify the meaning of the underlined word. Use a dictionary to check the meaning you inferred.

1. The garage is full of <u>debris</u>; similarly, the attic is _____
   _____

2. Jean said the tiny stain on the tablecloth was as <u>minuscule</u> as _____
   _____

3. Vince knew by the <u>stern</u> look on her face that something was wrong; Ed looked
   similarly _____

Writer's Choice: Vocabulary and Spelling Strategies and Practice, Grade 6   17

Vocabulary and Spelling Strategies and Practice

Name .... Class .... Date ....

18 Learning from Context: Comparison II

> **Key Information**
>
> When you find an unfamiliar word, look at the surrounding words and sentences, or context. You may find a clue to the word's meaning. Sometimes the writer compares the unfamiliar word to something familiar, as in this sentence.
>
> Kevin was *amiable* at the party; Katrina was also friendly.
>
> The word *also* suggests a comparison is being made. From this comparison you could guess that *amiable* means "friendly." Here are two words writers often use when making comparisons.
>
> likewise   also

■ A. Relating Familiar and Unfamiliar Words

In each sentence, circle the word that introduces a comparison. Then write the underlined word and its meaning. Check your answers in a dictionary.

1. The path of the earth around the sun is an <u>ellipse</u>; likewise, each of the other planets travels in an oval path. _____

2. Hattie was in a <u>somber</u> mood at the meeting; Jim was also feeling sad. _____

3. Ethan became <u>restless</u> while waiting for his father to arrive; likewise, his brother Jason couldn't sit still. _____

4. Jo saw an otter <u>slither</u> down the muddy bank into the stream; she also saw a muskrat slide down the bank. _____

■ B. Using Words in Sentences

Use each word below in a sentence. In your sentence compare the unfamiliar word to something familiar, using the clue word provided. Check your use of the word against the dictionary.

1. idolize (also)

   _____

2. apparel (likewise)

   _____

Vocabulary and Spelling Strategies and Practice

Name .... Class .... Date ....

19 Learning from Context: Contrast I

Key Information

When you come across an unfamiliar word while reading, see if there is a clue to the word's meaning in the surrounding words. In the following sentence, the writer contrasts the unfamiliar word with something familiar:

   The servants prepared a *lavish* feast for the king, but their own supper left them hungry.

The word *but* introduces a contrasting example. This word tells you the servants' supper was different from the king's supper. You know the servants had very little to eat, so you could guess that the king had plenty and that *lavish* means "plentiful." Here are some words that signal a contrast between two things.

   but   however

■ A. Figuring Out Word Meanings

Circle the clue words that signal contrast in the following sentences. Then use the contrasting example to figure out the meaning of the underlined word. Write the word and its meaning on the line. Then use a dictionary to check your answer.

1. The two countries were <u>hostile</u> toward each other in the past; today, however, they are on friendly terms. _____

2. A candle attracts moths, but the strong smell of cedar wood <u>repels</u> them. _____

3. On Tuesday Sam had a mild cold, but by Thursday his cold was so <u>severe</u> he had to stay in bed. _____

4. The characters in the movie were <u>fictional</u>; however, the historical events were real. _____

■ B. Writing Words in Sentences

Choose two of the underlined words you defined in Part A. Write an original sentence in which you use each word correctly.

1. _____

2. _____

Vocabulary and Spelling Strategies and Practice

Name .... Class .... Date ....

20 Learning from Context: Contrast II

> **Key Information**
>
> An unfamiliar word always appears with surrounding words that are probably familiar to you. Sometimes these surrounding words provide a clue to the meaning of the unfamiliar word. Consider this sentence:
>
> > The first speaker was concise in answering questions from the audience; on the other hand, the second speaker repeated herself and sometimes missed the point.
>
> The words *on the other hand* introduce a contrasting example. From the example you could guess that *concise* means "brief," or "to the point." A concise reply is the opposite of a wordy or vague one. Below are some words that indicate contrast.
>
> > unlike   on the other hand

■ A. Relating Familiar and Unfamiliar Words

Use the contrasting example to learn what the underlined word means. Then write the word and its meaning on the line. Check your answer against the dictionary.

1. Unlike the natural flowers, the <u>artificial</u> flowers had no scent. _____
   _____

2. The green lights on Lincoln Avenue helped us make good time; on the other hand, a fallen tree <u>hindered</u> our progress on Bell Street. _____
   _____

■ B. Using Words in Sentences

Complete each sentence so that the meaning of the underlined word becomes clear. Use a dictionary if necessary.

1. The signature on the document was <u>genuine</u>; on the other hand, the signature in the front of the book _____
   _____

2. Miguel has a <u>strenuous</u> job, so on weekends he is happy to _____
   _____

3. Unlike Marcy, who is _____, Elise has <u>slovenly</u> habits.

4. Players on the losing team _____ as they headed toward the locker room; the winning team, on the other hand, was <u>jubilant</u>.

20 Writer's Choice: Vocabulary and Spelling Strategies and Practice, Grade 6

Vocabulary and Spelling Strategies and Practice

Name .... Class .... Date ....

21 Word Parts: Roots I

Key Information

You can figure out the meaning of an unfamiliar word by dividing it into parts. The main part of a word is called the root. It carries the word's basic meaning. Often, the root is not a complete word. Many such roots, like those below, are borrowed from the ancient Latin language.

Root	Meaning	Example	Meaning of Word
scrib, scrip	write	inscribe	to write in
dic	say or speak	predict	foretell

Prefixes and suffixes can be attached to a root to make its meaning more specific. To predict (pre- + dict) means to tell about something before it happens, or foretell.

A. Building Words from Roots

Write all the words from the list that share one of the roots shown.

scribe   description   contradict   scribble
dictate   manuscript   dictionary   transcribe

1. scrib, scrip (write)

_____
_____
_____
_____

2. dic (speak, say)

_____
_____
_____
_____

B. Using Words in Sentences

Complete each sentence, using a word from the list in Part A. Use a dictionary as needed.

1. Raul had only a few seconds to _____ the instructions.
2. Michelle decided to _____ a poem in the book she gave to her father.
3. Some creative people _____ their ideas into a tape recorder while they walk or ride.
4. The author's _____ was difficult to read because she had erased and revised it so many times.
5. In medieval times the job of a _____ involved copying entire books by hand.

Writer's Choice: Vocabulary and Spelling Strategies and Practice, Grade 6   **21**

Vocabulary and Spelling Strategies and Practice

Name .... Class .... Date ....

22 Word Parts: Roots II

Key Information

The main part of a word is its root. When a prefix or suffix is added to a root, the new word takes its meaning from all the word parts. But the main meaning of the word comes from the root. The chart below shows some common roots that come from Latin.

Root	Meaning	Example	Meaning of Word
port	carry	report	tell (carry back information)
fin	end	finish	bring to an end
vid, vis	see	vision	sight

■ A. Combining Word Parts

Combine the word parts below to form a word. Be sure each root carries the meaning shown in the box above. Write the new word and its meaning on the lines below. Use a dictionary if you need help.

Word Parts   Complete Word   Meaning

1. ex- + port =   _____   _____

2. in- + fin + -ite = _____   _____

3. vis + -ible =   _____   _____

4. e- + vid + -ent =   _____   _____

■ B. Analyzing Word Parts

Complete each sentence using a word from the list below.

   final   porter   export   evidence
   infinite   transportation   video   define

1. The night sky is so vast that the heavens look _____.

2. The Dominican Republic, a country in the Caribbean Sea, continues to _____ most of its sugar to the United States.

3. As a wise clown spoke the _____ words of the play, the curtain began to come down.

4. Our neighbor built a fence to _____ the boundaries of his back yard.

5. The _____ brought the baggage into the hotel lobby.

6. Two of the more modern forms of _____ are hovercraft and monorail.

7. Panjit adjusted the _____ on the computer monitor because the screen was too dark.

8. The detectives looked for _____ at the scene of the crime.

Vocabulary and Spelling Strategies and Practice

Name .... Class .... Date ....

23 Word Parts: Prefixes I

Key Information

A prefix is a word part that is added to the beginning of a root. Sometimes a prefix can completely change the meaning of the root. Both of the prefixes below have the meaning "not" or "opposite of."

Prefix	Meaning	Example	Meaning
un-	not, opposite of	unfair untie	not fair to loosen
dis-	not, opposite of	disorder disagree	lack of order to not agree

■ A. Adding Prefixes

Add the correct prefix meaning "not" to each word. The result will be a word that means the opposite of the word provided. For cases in which both *un-* and *dis-* can be used to create a new word, explain how the two words differ in meaning. Check your answers in a dictionary.

1. ripe _____
2. able _____
3. do _____
4. continue _____
5. sophisticated _____
6. honest _____
7. willing _____
8. approve _____
9. like _____
10. courteous _____

■ B. Writing Definitions

Circle the prefix that has been added to each word below. Then write a brief definition of each complete word. Check your answers in a dictionary.

1. disadvantage _____
2. ungrateful _____
3. unleash _____
4. disbelief _____
5. disconnect _____

Writer's Choice: Vocabulary and Spelling Strategies and Practice, Grade 6   23

Vocabulary and Spelling Strategies and Practice

Name .... Class .... Date ....

24 Word Parts: Prefixes II

Key Information

A prefix is a word part that is added to the beginning of a root. Listed below are two more prefixes that reverse the meaning of the root.

Prefix	Meaning	Example	Meaning
non-	not	nondairy	without milk
in-	opposite of	involuntary	not voluntary

■ A. Defining Words

Circle the prefix in each word. Then write a brief definition of the complete word.

1. insincere _____
2. nonfatal _____
3. inflexible _____
4. nonstop _____
5. nonresident _____
6. inactive _____

■ B. Matching Words with Meanings

Match the correct word or phrase from this list with each example given, and write the answer on the line. You may need to check meanings in a dictionary.

    involuntary reaction   nonsense   inhospitable conditions
    nondairy product   noncombatant   nonmechanical toy

1. coffee "cream" made from soybean and coconut oil
   _____

2. a desert without water, shade, or food
   _____

3. a soldier whose duties do not include fighting in battle
   _____

4. a fleeble zirkpot
   _____

5. the kick of a dangling leg when a doctor taps it below the kneecap
   _____

6. a teddy bear
   _____

24 Writer's Choice: Vocabulary and Spelling Strategies and Practice, Grade 6

Vocabulary and Spelling Strategies and Practice

Name .... Class .... Date ....

25 Word Parts: Prefixes III

Key Information

A word part attached before a root is called a prefix. Two common prefixes are *pre-* and *de-*. Below are some examples of words with these prefixes.

Prefix	Meaning	Example	Meaning
pre-	before	preview	to view in advance
		prejudge	to judge in advance
		pregame	before a game
de-	remove or reduce	defrost	to remove frost
		dehydrate	to reduce or remove water
		debug	to remove errors

■ A. Using Words in Sentences

Complete each sentence with a word from the chart above.

1. The software designer stayed up all night to _____ the computer program.
2. During the _____ meeting the coaches went over the rules.
3. No one volunteered to _____ the freezer when it was empty.
4. Staying out in the hot sun all day will _____ almost anyone.
5. To _____ is to form an opinion about something before giving it careful thought.

■ B. Using Words Correctly

Match the correct word from the list with each clue below. Use a dictionary as needed.

    precolonial   descend
    deprived   prerecorded

1. Occurring before a country was settled by outsiders _____
2. To go from the top to the bottom of a staircase _____
3. How you might feel if your allowance was taken away _____
4. Describing a radio broadcast that is not live _____

Writer's Choice: Vocabulary and Spelling Strategies and Practice, Grade 6

Vocabulary and Spelling Strategies and Practice

Name .... Class .... Date ....

26   Word Parts: Suffixes I

> **Key Information**
>
> A suffix is a word part added at the end of a root. Adding a suffix often changes a word's part of speech as well as its meaning. For example, adding *-er* to *train* (a verb) makes *trainer* (a noun). The suffixes *-er*, *-or*, and *-ist* all mean "one who."
>
> | Suffix | Meaning | Word | Meaning |
> |--------|---------|------|---------|
> | -er | one who | trainer | one who trains |
> | -or | one who | conductor | one who conducts |
> | -ist | one who | artist | one who creates art |

■ A. Writing Definitions

Circle the suffix in each word. Then write a definition in your own words. Refer to a dictionary as needed.

1. employer _____
2. collector _____
3. editor _____
4. canoeist _____
5. inventor _____
6. scientist _____
7. spectator _____
8. dictator _____
9. supervisor _____
10. consumer _____

■ B. Noticing Suffixes

Read each sentence. Then write the words that include the suffix *-or*, *-er*, or *-ist*.

1. The governor of our state is a former U.S. senator.
   _____

2. The manager of the grocery store is also an inventor.
   _____

3. Among the spectators were sailors, canoeists, and skiers.
   _____

4. The editor changed the word *treasurer* to *tax collector*.
   _____

5. The orchestra conductor nodded to the pianist.
   _____

Vocabulary and Spelling Strategies and Practice

Name .... Class .... Date ....

27 Word Parts: Suffixes II

Key Information

A suffix is a word part added at the end of a root. Adding a suffix often changes a word's part of speech as well as its meaning. For example, adding -*able* to *wash* (a verb) makes *washable* (an adjective). Two suffixes that form adjectives are -*able* and -*ible*. Both suffixes mean "can be" or "having the quality of."

Suffix	Meaning	Word	Meaning
-able	can be, having the quality of	washable comfortable	can be washed having comfort
-ible	can be, having the quality of	sensible digestible	having sense can be digested

■ A. Writing Definitions

For each word that includes the suffix -*able* or -*ible*, write down the word's root. Then write a definition of the whole word. Remember that a prefix is not part of the root. Consult a dictionary as needed.

1. The water is not drinkable directly from the stream, but it is treatable.
   _____

2. The fashionable dress had an incredible collar that stuck out like a platter.
   _____

3. The dog enjoys riding in the convertible, but taking her off the leash during a ride would be unthinkable. _____
   _____

4. The winds are favorable for the voyage, but the leaky sailboat is not dependable.
   _____

5. It is not sensible to shoot at a target that is not visible.
   _____

■ B. Matching Words to Definitions

On the line write the word that fits the definition given. The words you write should end in -*able* or -*ible*. Then use a dictionary to check your spellings.

1. Food that can be digested _____
2. Advice that makes sense _____
3. A sign that can be read _____
4. A story you can believe _____
5. A couch that can be converted into a bed _____

Writer's Choice: Vocabulary and Spelling Strategies and Practice, Grade 6   **27**

Vocabulary and Spelling Strategies and Practice

Name .... Class .... Date ....

28 Word Parts: Suffixes III

Key Information

A suffix often changes a word's part of speech as well as its meaning. For example, adding -less to hair (a noun) makes hairless (an adjective). Adding -ness to happy (an adjective) makes happiness (a noun). Some words formed by adding these two suffixes are shown below.

Suffix	Meaning	Example	Meaning
-less	without	spineless	without a spine
		colorless	without color
-ness	having the quality or state of being	mildness	quality of being mild
		loneliness	state of being lonely

■ A. Adding Suffixes

Divide each word into its parts. Then write the meaning of the word.

Word	=	Root	+	Suffix	Meaning
1. stillness		_____	+	_____	_____
2. humorless		_____	+	_____	_____
3. wireless		_____	+	_____	_____
4. gentleness		_____	+	_____	_____
5. penniless		_____	+	_____	_____

■ B. Drawing Conclusions About Words

Answer each question with *yes* or *no*. Then briefly explain your answer. Do not use a root of the underlined word in your response. Consult a dictionary as needed.

Example: Could a dancer be graceless?
Response: Yes—if the dancer is awkward or clumsy.

1. Could a radio be cordless?
   _____

2. Could a runner be tireless?
   _____

3. Could a person be humorless?
   _____

4. Could an expedition be fruitless?
   _____

28 Writer's Choice: Vocabulary and Spelling Strategies and Practice, Grade 6

Vocabulary and Spelling Strategies and Practice

Name .... Class .... Date ....

29 Word Relationships: Synonyms I

Key Information

Words with similar meanings are called synonyms. For example, *consume* and *devour* both mean "eat." These words, however, do not have exactly the same meaning. *Consume* means simply "to take in food," whereas *devour* means "to eat greedily." A reference book that lists synonyms is called a thesaurus.

Synonyms	More Exact Meanings
riddle	word puzzle
mystery	event with no explanation
picture	any image showing an object
photograph	an image obtained using camera and film

■ A. Finding Synonyms

List two synonyms for each word below. Use a dictionary or thesaurus if necessary.

1. car, _____, _____
2. eager, _____, _____
3. ponder, _____, _____
4. durable, _____, _____
5. glide, _____, _____

■ B. Using Synonyms in Sentences

Read each sentence. Then cross out the underlined word, and write a synonym for it on the line. Consult a dictionary if you need help.

1. Her cheeks were <u>ruddy</u> from leaning close to the fire.
   _____

2. The driver missed the exit because he was <u>bewildered</u> by all the freeway signs.
   _____

3. Several passengers became seasick on the <u>tempestuous</u> voyage.
   _____

4. Nguyen <u>reprimanded</u> his little sister for running across the street.
   _____

5. The other group members were <u>perturbed</u> when Sheila refused to do any research.
   _____

Writer's Choice: Vocabulary and Spelling Strategies and Practice, Grade 6

Vocabulary and Spelling Strategies and Practice

Name .... Class .... Date ....

30 Word Relationships: Synonyms II

Key Information

Synonyms are words with similar meanings. Some synonyms, such as *try* and *attempt*, have almost exactly the same meaning. Many other synonyms have somewhat different meanings. For example, a *joke* is something said or done to provoke laughter, and a *wisecrack* is a clever but insensitive remark. Writers must be careful to choose the exact word they mean.

■ A. Linking Familiar and Unfamiliar Words

Match each word with a synonym from the list. Use a dictionary or thesaurus as needed.

| incorrect | pliable | surly | lucid | grueling |
| sufficient | leery | severe | tranquil | awkward |

1. clumsy _____
2. stern _____
3. distrustful _____
4. flexible _____
5. clear _____
6. tiring _____
7. gruff _____
8. enough _____
9. wrong _____
10. peaceful _____

■ B. Grouping Synonyms

For each item write three synonyms from the list. Consult a dictionary if you need help.

| babble | shimmer | stroll | glimmer | chatter |
| amble | jabber | glitter | saunter | |

1. to walk at a leisurely pace

   _____   _____   _____

2. to talk quickly or idly

   _____   _____   _____

3. to shine with bright flashes

   _____   _____   _____

Writer's Choice: Vocabulary and Spelling Strategies and Practice, Grade 6

Vocabulary and Spelling Strategies and Practice

Name .... Class .... Date ....

31 Word Relationships: Antonyms I

> **Key Information**
>
> Words with opposite or nearly opposite meanings are called antonyms. For example, *cold* is an antonym of *hot*. Knowing antonyms can help you understand the meanings of other words and can help you build your vocabulary.
>
> | Word | Antonym |
> |---|---|
> | weaken | strengthen |
> | stormy | calm |

■ A. Linking Familiar and Unfamiliar Words

Match each word with an antonym from the list. Use a dictionary or thesaurus as needed.

    severe   courteous   artificial   taciturn   sweltering
    ruddy   silly   authentic   energetic   prompt

1. solemn _____
2. mild _____
3. natural _____
4. talkative _____
5. lifeless _____
6. pale _____
7. tardy _____
8. rude _____
9. fake _____
10. frigid _____

■ B. Using Antonyms in Sentences

Complete each sentence, using a pair of antonyms from Part A.

1. Summer days in Minnesota can be _____, but the winters can be _____.

2. The cub scouts were _____ during the flag ceremony, but later, when they practiced tongue-twisters, they became _____.

3. The collector looked at the 1928 dollar bill with a magnifying glass to make sure it was _____, that is, not _____.

4. Lynnelle is _____ by nature, but she was so _____ at the party that her voice became hoarse.

5. Alex is usually _____, but he was _____ today because the school bus had a flat tire.

Writer's Choice: Vocabulary and Spelling Strategies and Practice, Grade 6   **31**

Vocabulary and Spelling Strategies and Practice

Name .... Class .... Date ....

32 Word Relationships: Antonyms II

Key Information

Words that have opposite or nearly opposite meanings from each other are called antonyms. Antonyms can sometimes be formed by adding a prefix meaning "not" or "the opposite of" to a word. For example, you can make an antonym of *true* by adding the prefix *un-*.

Word	+	Prefix	=	Antonym
bind		un-		unbind
credible		in-		incredible
pleasure		dis-		displeasure
vocal		non-		nonvocal

■ A. Forming Antonyms

Write an antonym for each word by adding the correct prefix from the list. Check your answers in a dictionary.

       un-   in-   non-   dis-

1. advantage _____
2. conformist _____
3. exceptional _____
4. embarrassed _____
5. allergic _____
6. belief _____
7. courteous _____
8. grammatical _____
9. exact _____
10. firm _____

■ B. Using Antonyms in Sentences

Create an antonym from the underlined word by adding a prefix that means "not." Use *un-*, *in-*, or *non-*. Then use each new phrase in a sentence. Check each antonym in a dictionary to make sure you have used the correct prefix.

1. a <u>musical</u> sound; an _____ sound
   _____

2. a <u>complete</u> set; an _____ set
   _____

3. a <u>technical</u> word; a _____ word
   _____

Vocabulary and Spelling Strategies and Practice

Name .... Class .... Date ....

33 Word Relationships: Homonyms

Key Information

Homonyms are words that sound alike but have different meanings. Most homonyms, such as *brake* and *break,* are spelled differently. The chart below shows some examples of homonyms.

Word	Meaning	Word	Meaning
their	belonging to them	hear	listen
there	in that place	here	this place
they're	contraction of *they are*		
		to	in the direction of
its	belonging to it	too	also
it's	contraction of *it is* or *it has*	two	the number 2
your	belonging to you	principle	a rule, law, or truth
you're	contraction of *you are*	principal	the head of a school; most important

■ A. Spotting Incorrect Words

Each phrase below contains an incorrectly used word. Cross out the word. Then write the phrase using the correct word. Refer to the chart above.

1. over there heads _____
2. when your finished _____
3. they're own house _____
4. it's own batteries _____
5. you're first visit _____

■ B. Using Words in Sentences

Complete each sentence with the correct word from the chart.

1. Lily nodded and said, "I agree with you; I think so, _____."
2. The _____ cause of lung cancer is smoking.
3. The ranger pointed at his feet and said, "Start _____ if you want to take the nature walk."
4. A _____ of American democracy is "one person, one vote."
5. Raphael mapped out _____ different routes on the map; we chose the shorter one.

Writer's Choice: Vocabulary and Spelling Strategies and Practice, Grade 6

Vocabulary and Spelling Strategies and Practice

Name .... Class .... Date ....

34 Word Relationships: Borrowed Words

Key Information

Many words in the English language are borrowed directly or indirectly from other languages. For example, *banjo* comes from an African language. *Tornado* comes from Spanish, *umbrella* from Italian, and *zero* from Arabic.

■ A. Identifying Borrowed Words

Use the dictionary to match each word with the language or language group in which it first appeared. One extra language is listed.

Greek	Irish	German
Taino	French	West African
Arabic	Latin	Old English
Hindi	Old Norse	

1. shampoo _____
2. plow _____
3. algebra _____
4. jukebox _____
5. dollar _____
6. hurricane _____
7. empire _____
8. democracy _____
9. oaf _____
10. galore _____

■ B. Linking Words and Definitions

Write the word from the list that fits each definition. A language clue is given after the definition. Check your answers against the dictionary.

    honcho   moccasin   blitz   café   parent

1. one who begets a child (Latin) _____
2. a slipper made of soft, flexible leather (Algonquian) _____
3. place to get coffee and other drinks and snacks (Italian) _____
4. a bigshot or boss (Japanese) _____
5. a sudden, overwhelming attack, like lightning (German) _____

34 Writer's Choice: Vocabulary and Spelling Strategies and Practice, Grade 6

Vocabulary and Spelling Strategies and Practice

Name .... Class .... Date ....

35 Using a Dictionary I

Key Information

Many words have more than one meaning. Notice the word *roll* in each of the following sentences.

> The coin began to roll across the table.
> Amiri bought a cinnamon roll at the bakery.
> At the start of class, the teacher called the roll.

As a verb, the word *roll* can mean "to move by turning over and over." As a noun, it can mean "a small piece of baked dough" or "a list of names of the members of a group." When you look up a word in the dictionary, be sure to read all of its meanings.

■ A. Noticing Different Meanings

Use a dictionary to write two different meanings for each word. After the meaning, note whether the word, as defined, is a noun or a verb.

1. hamper

    a. _____

    b. _____

2. rattle

    a. _____

    b. _____

■ B. Using Words in Sentences

Read each sentence, and think about the meaning of the underlined word. Then write another sentence that uses the same word but with a different meaning. You may want to add a word ending such as *-ed* or *-s*.

1. The carpenter used a hand drill to bore a hole in the wood.

    _____

2. She signed the report card with a ballpoint pen.

    _____

3. The image on the movie screen was out of focus.

    _____

4. They sat in front of the crackling fire, feeling very content.

    _____

Writer's Choice: Vocabulary and Spelling Strategies and Practice, Grade 6

Vocabulary and Spelling Strategies and Practice

Name .... Class .... Date ....

36 Using a Dictionary II

> **Key Information**
>
> In a dictionary, the pronunciation follows the entry word. The letters and symbols in the pronunciation stand for different sounds. If you are not sure how to say the sounds, you can use the pronunciation key at the bottom of the dictionary page. The key below shows how the letters and symbols sound in short, familiar words.
>
> | a | at | ī | ice | ou | out | zh | treasure |
> |---|---|---|---|---|---|---|---|
> | ā | ape | o | hot | u | up | ə | about |
> | ä | car | ō | old | ū | use | ə | taken |
> | e | end | ô | fork | ur | turn | ə | pencil |
> | ē | me | oo | book | th | thin | ə | lemon |
> | i | it | o͞o | boot | th | this | ə | circus |
>
> For example, *fragile* can be said in two ways: fraj′əl or fraj′īl. You can pronounce the *i* like the *i* in *pencil* or like the *i* in *ice*.

■ A. Pronouncing Words

Match each pronunciation with a word from the list. Then say the word out loud.

    rhythm   aviation   ridicule   convex   quirky   dubious

1. kon veks′ _____   **4.** rid′ ə kūl′ _____

2. do͞o′ bē əs _____   **5.** ri**th**′ əm _____

3. kwur′ kē _____   **6.** ā′ vē ā′ shən _____

■ B. Understanding Pronunciations

Use a dictionary to answer each question in a short sentence. Consult a pronunciation key as needed.

1. Is the *t* in *duct* pronounced or silent? _____

2. Does the *i* in *igloo* sound like the *i* in *ride* or in *pit*? _____

3. Does *cello* begin with the same sound as *cellar* or as *church*? _____

4. Does the first *i* in *ibis* rhyme with *by*? _____

5. Do *bread* and *knead* rhyme? _____

6. Are *hanger* and *hangar* pronounced the same? _____

Writer's Choice: Vocabulary and Spelling Strategies and Practice, Grade 6

Vocabulary and Spelling Strategies and Practice

Name .... Class .... Date ....

37   Using a Dictionary III

> **Key Information**
>
> A dictionary entry sometimes lists synonyms. The list will help you understand the entry word better. The explanations will help you clarify some important differences among the synonyms.
>
>   **hole** (hōl) *noun* [Middle English *hol(e)*, hole, ship's hold, from Old English *hol*, hollow place] a cavity in something solid
>   Synonyms: *hole, hollow, excavation, cave.* These nouns refer to an unfilled space in an otherwise solid body. *Hole* refers to any opening in or through a solid object. *Hollow* refers to either an untilled area or a surface depression in a solid body, such as a valley. *Excavation* refers to any human-made hole. A *cave* is a hollow, or empty chamber, in the earth.

■ A. Using Synonyms in Sentences

Replace the underlined word with a synonym that makes the sentence more accurate. Refer to a dictionary as needed.

1. A bulldozer made a <u>hole</u> for the basement of her new house. _____
2. The ranger entered the <u>hole</u> by the waterfall to walk to the underground stream. _____
3. "Bicycling is my favorite <u>amusement</u>," said Sarah. _____
4. He could run the machine after he got some <u>education</u> for it. _____
5. The supply of crackers for the party was <u>ample</u>; two unopened boxes were left over. _____

■ B. Finding Synonyms

Use a dictionary to find two synonyms for each word.

1. deceive _____ _____
2. stumble _____ _____
3. break _____ _____
4. tired _____ _____
5. calm _____ _____

Writer's Choice: Vocabulary and Spelling Strategies and Practice, Grade 6

Vocabulary and Spelling Strategies and Practice

Name .... Class .... Date ....

38 Using a Dictionary IV

> **Key Information**
>
> A dictionary entry can answer questions about the meaning, spelling, and pronunciation of a word. The entry also tells what part of speech a word is and gives the word's origin, if it is known.
>
> **garnish** (gär′nish) *verb* [Middle English *garnischen*, to equip, adorn, from Old French *garnir*] to decorate food with something that adds color or flavor
>
> **garrison** (gār′ə sən′) *noun* [Middle English *garison*, protection, fortress, from Old French *garison*] a place where soldiers are stationed; a military post
>
> **garter** (gär′tər) *noun* [Old Norman French *gartier*, from Old French *garet*, the bend of the knee] a band worn around the leg to hold up a stocking or sock
>
> **garter snake** a nonpoisonous snake of North America, green and brown with long yellow stripes

■ A. Understanding Definitions

Complete each sentence with one of the words listed above. In one sentence the form of the word must be changed.

1. When the knight removed the _____ from each leg, his stockings sagged around his ankles.
2. Many people _____ fish with slices of lemon and sprigs of parsley.
3. Paula's little sister held up a _____ that she found in the garden.
4. More than four hundred soldiers could be housed at the _____.
5. The telephone rang just as he was _____ the salad with chives.

■ B. Understanding Word Entries

Use the entries above to answer each question.

1. Which word is a synonym for *embellish*? _____
2. Are garter snakes dangerous? Why or why not?

   _____

3. Is the first syllable of *garter* pronounced the same as the first syllable of *garnish* or of *garrison*? _____

4. Which words have their origin in Old French or in Old Norman French?

   _____

5. *Garter* comes from the Old French word *garet*. What is the meaning of *garet*?

   _____

Vocabulary and Spelling Strategies and Practice

Name .... Class .... Date ....

39 | Using a Dictionary V

Key Information

Many words can be used as more than one part of speech. In a dictionary you will often find separate entries for each part of speech, as in the entry below.

master (mas′tər) *noun* [Latin *magister,* akin to Latin *magnus,* great] **1.** A person who has power or control over something **2.** A person of great learning, skill, or ability **3.** A male teacher or tutor, especially one at a private school **4.** An old-fashioned term for a boy too young to be called *mister;* used as a title—*adjective* **1.** Highly skilled; expert **2.** Most important; main—*verb* **1.** To gain control over; overcome **2.** To become expert in

■ A. Understanding Definitions

Refer to the dictionary entry above to write the correct meaning of each underlined word.

1. The dog always responded to the commands of its <u>master</u>.

   _____

2. Janette's father is a <u>master</u> carpenter.

   _____

3. Peter is trying to <u>master</u> the ability to walk on stilts.

   _____

4. The Dutch artist Rembrandt was one of the great <u>masters</u> of oil painting.

   _____

5. Amelia pulled the <u>master</u> list out of her desk.

   _____

■ B. Understanding Word Entries

Refer to the entry above to complete the exercises.

1. From what language or languages is the word *master* borrowed?

   _____

2. Write an original sentence in which *master* is used as a verb.

   _____

3. Write an original sentence in which *master* is used as an adjective.

   _____

4. Write an original sentence in which *master* is used as a noun.

   _____

Writer's Choice: Vocabulary and Spelling Strategies and Practice, Grade 6

Vocabulary and Spelling Strategies and Practice

40 Using a Dictionary VI

> **Key Information**
>
> Have you ever had the experience of looking up one word and being distracted by another? Maybe you came across a funny-sounding word and wondered what it meant. Or perhaps a picture for a word made you curious about its meaning. A dictionary is a fun place to make discoveries about words.

■ A. Making Word Discoveries

You probably know that a group of goats is called a herd. But have you ever heard of a clowder of cats? Each word in the list below refers to a group of specific animals. Use a standard desk dictionary to find the right word for each kind of animal.

   pride   gaggle   litter   bevy   swarm

1. a _____ of geese
2. a _____ of bees
3. a _____ of lions
4. a _____ of quail
5. a _____ of puppies

■ B. Exploring Words

Use a dictionary to answer the following questions.

1. From what language did English borrow the word *cookie*?

2. How is the word *dromedary* divided into syllables?

3. What is a another word for *prevail*?

4. Is *rile* a noun or a verb?

5. How is *ti* pronounced in the word *ambitious*? Give an example of another word in which *ti* is pronounced the same way.

6. Does the word *maize*, meaning "corn," rhyme with *size*, *daze*, or *sneeze*?

Vocabulary and Spelling Strategies and Practice

Name .... Class .... Date ....

41 Spelling Rules: *ie* and *ei*

Key Information

The rhyming rule below can help you remember when to use *ie* and when to use *ei*. Some common exceptions to the rule are also listed.

Rhyming Rule
Put *i* before *e*
except after *c*
or when sounded like *a*,
as in *neighbor* and *weigh*.

Examples
believe, chief, grieve
receive, ceiling, receipt

eight, weight, veil, freight

Some exceptions to the *ie* and *ei* rule
species, seize, leisure, weird, either, neither, height

■ A. Spotting Spelling Errors

In each set of words, circle the incorrectly spelled word. Then spell the word correctly on the line.

1. neigh, believe, liesure _____
2. greive, siege, receipt _____
3. ceiling, speceis, seize _____
4. field, weight, frieght _____
5. height, neither, wierd _____

■ B. Writing *ei* and *ie* Words in Sentences

Write an original sentence to illustrate each spelling rule. Use any of the appropriate words in the box or use others you know.

1. *ei* after *c*

   _____

2. *ie*, not after *c*

   _____

3. *ei*, when sounded like *a*, as in *weigh*

   _____

4. exceptions to the *ie/ei* rule

   _____

Vocabulary and Spelling Strategies and Practice

Name .... Class .... Date ....

42 Spelling Rules: Suffixes and the Silent *e*

Key Information

Many words end in silent *e*. When you add a suffix to such words, you sometimes drop the *e*. Follow these rules to figure out when to keep the *e* and when to drop it.

Keep the *e* when
- the word ends in silent *e*
  <u>and</u> the suffix begins with a consonant.

- the word ends in *ce* or *ge*
  <u>and</u> the suffix begins with *a* or *o*.

- the word ends in *ee* or *oe*
  <u>and</u> the suffix begins with a vowel.

Drop the *e* when
- the word ends in silent *e*
  <u>and</u> the suffix begins with a vowel.

Examples
pure + -ly = purely
<u>Exception:</u> awe + -ful = awful

trace + -able = traceable
change + -able = changeable
courage + ous = courageous

agree + -ing = agreeing
hoe + -ing = hoeing

shine + -y = shiny
write + -ing = writing
<u>Exception:</u> dye + -ing = dyeing

■ A. Combining Word Parts

Correctly spell each new word.

1. fame + -ous = _____
2. care + -ful = _____
3. shine + -y = _____
4. hoe + -ing = _____
5. fine + -est = _____
6. manage + -able = _____
7. outrage + -ous = _____
8. dodge + -ing = _____

■ B. Spotting Spelling Errors

In each pair of words, circle the incorrectly spelled word. Then spell the word correctly on the line.

1. fakeing, raking
   _____
2. exciteable, believable
   _____
3. hasty, tastey
   _____
4. manageable, changable
   _____
5. seeing, agreing
   _____
6. peacable, peaceful
   _____
7. rarely, completly
   _____
8. budging, judgeing
   _____

Vocabulary and Spelling Strategies and Practice

Name .... Class .... Date ....

43 Spelling Rules: Suffixes and the Final *y*

Key Information

When adding a suffix to a word ending in *y*, follow these rules.

Change *y* to *i* when
there is a consonant before the *y*.

Examples
cry + -ed = cried
carry + -ed = carried

Exception: Keep the *y* when
the suffix begins with an *i*.

carry + -ing = carrying

Keep the *y* when
there is a vowel before the *y*.

Examples
play + -ful = playful
enjoy + -ing = enjoying

■ A. Using Words in Sentences

Complete each sentence by combining the root word and the suffix.

1. Jan _____ but could not budge the piano an inch. (try + -ed)
2. Admission to the craft show is _____ at the door. (pay +-able)
3. The fur of the orange cat is _____ than the white cat's fur. (fluffy + -er)
4. Jill and Whitney _____ the mystery about the Loch Ness monster. (enjoy + -ed)
5. Phil was _____ the table when the guests arrived. (ready + -ing)

■ B. Spotting Spelling Errors

In each pair of words, circle the incorrectly spelled word. Then spell the word correctly on the line.

1. studying, copiing _____
2. fuzzyer, joyful _____
3. tarryed, stayed _____
4. married, hurriing _____
5. holyness, surveying _____

Vocabulary and Spelling Strategies and Practice

Name .... Class .... Date ....

44 Spelling Rules: Doubling the Final Consonant

Key Information

Follow these rules for doubling the final consonant when adding a suffix:

Double the final consonant when one vowel comes before the consonant <u>and</u>

- the word has only one syllable.
- the word has an accent on the last syllable that remains there after the suffix is added.

Example

sit + -ing = sitting
prefer + -ed = preferred
control + -ing = controlling

Do not double the final consonant when
- the suffix begins with a consonant.
- the accent is not on the last syllable.
- the accent moves to another syllable when the suffix is added.
- two vowels come before the final consonant.
- the word ends in two consonants.

Example

pain + -less = painless
offer + -ed = offered
refer + -ence = reference

moan + -ed = moaned
remind + -er = reminder

■ A. Combining Word Parts

Correctly spell each new word.

1. prefer + -ence = _____
2. submit + -ed = _____
3. snack + -ing = _____
4. forget + -ful = _____
5. plan + -ed = _____

■ B. Finding Spelling Errors

Find the one misspelled word in each sentence. Then spell the word correctly on the line.

1. Wind whiped the tattered flag. _____
2. The athlete was pained by the trainning session. _____
3. The lawyer regreted forgetting her briefcase. _____
4. Both librarians offerred a reference book. _____
5. The drifting snow reminded him of sand dunes. _____

Writer's Choice: Vocabulary and Spelling Strategies and Practice, Grade 6

Vocabulary and Spelling Strategies and Practice

Name .... Class .... Date ....

45 Spelling Rules: Forming Compound Words

Key Information

A compound word is formed by joining two words. When forming compounds, keep the exact spelling of both words.

    green + house = greenhouse   sky + dive = skydive
    movie + goer = moviegoer   crafts + woman = craftswoman

■ A. Combining Words to Make Compounds

Match each description with a word from the list.

    kickstand   homespun   skywrite   kickoff
    seafarer   fairground   eyedropper   skyscraper

1. This marks the start of a football game. _____

2. Without this a bike will fall over. _____

3. Early settlers wove this coarse fabric. _____

4. Some airplanes can do this. _____

5. You might find a Ferris wheel here. _____

6. Christopher Columbus was one. _____

7. This building tickles the clouds. _____

8. A chemist might use this small tool. _____

■ B. Using Words in Sentences

Make a compound by combining each word below with a word from the following list. Then write a sentence using the compound correctly. Refer to a dictionary as needed.

    skate   cake   mobile   air

1. book + _____

_____

2. fruit + _____

_____

3. _____ + mail

_____

4. _____ + board

_____

Writer's Choice: Vocabulary and Spelling Strategies and Practice, Grade 6   **45**

Vocabulary and Spelling Strategies and Practice

Name .... Class .... Date ....

46 Spelling Rules: General Rules for Forming Plurals

Key Information

When forming the plural of a noun, follow these rules.

If the noun ends in	The rule is	Example
s, ch, sh, x, or z	Add -es	bus → buses
		church → churches
		tax → taxes
a consonant + y	Change y to i and add -es	baby → babies
		army → armies
a vowel + y	Add -s	day → days
a vowel + o	Add -s	stereo → stereos
a consonant + o	Add -s (usually)	photo → photos
	Exception:	hero → heroes
f or ff	Add -s (usually)	reef → reefs
	Exception:	leaf → leaves
lf	Change f to v and add -es	half → halves
		wolf → wolves
fe	Change f to v and add -s	life → lives
		knife → knives

■ A. Adding Plural Endings

Write the correct plural of each word. Check your answers in a dictionary.

1. journey _____
2. rodeo _____
3. cross _____
4. elf _____
5. swatch _____
6. solo _____
7. dish _____
8. dairy _____
9. tiff _____
10. fax _____

■ B. Spotting Spelling Errors

Circle the misspelled word in each set of plurals. Then spell the word correctly.

1. pianos, heros, wives _____
2. toys, wayes, delays _____
3. halfs, candies, cavities _____
4. jetties, videos, churchs _____

46 Writer's Choice: Vocabulary and Spelling Strategies and Practice, Grade 6

Vocabulary and Spelling Strategies and Practice

Name .... Class .... Date ....

47 Spelling Rules: Special Rules for Forming Plurals I

Key Information

The following rules cover special groups of words.

Word Group	Rule	Example
Proper names	Add -s to most names	Giordano → Giordanos Darcy → Darcys
	Add -es if the name ends in s, ch, sh, x, or z	Jones → Joneses Hatch → Hatches Marx → Marxes Valdez → Valdezes
Exception:	Add -s if the final ch is sounded like k	Bach → Bachs Murdoch → Murdochs
One-word compounds	Follow the general rules for plurals	teacup → teacups blackberry → blackberries
Hyphenated compounds	Make the most important word plural	runner-up → runners-up vice-president → vice-presidents

■ A. Using Plurals in Sentences

Complete each sentence by writing the plural of the underlined word.

1. The <u>Gomez</u> family was invited, but I don't see any of the _____ here.

2. This <u>textbook</u> is about geography; the other two _____ are about geology.

3. The <u>vice-president</u> spoke about the achievements of past _____.

4. Lee Anne has one <u>brother-in-law</u>, and Nathan has two _____.

5. Mrs. <u>March</u> arrived first, followed by all the other _____.

■ B. Spelling Plurals Correctly

Match each description with a word from the list. Write the plural of the word on the line.

runner-up   sweatshirt   lifeguard   icebox   editor-in-chief

1. People in charge of magazines _____
2. Old-fashioned refrigerators _____
3. People who come in second in a contest _____
4. Warm garments _____
5. People who look after swimmers _____

Writer's Choice: Vocabulary and Spelling Strategies and Practice, Grade 6

Vocabulary and Spelling Strategies and Practice

Name .... Class .... Date ....

48 Spelling Rules: Special Rules for Forming Plurals II

Key Information

Some words do not follow the usual rules in forming plurals.

Word Group	Examples
Nouns with irregular plurals	man → men
	ox → oxen
	child → children
	foot → feet
Nouns that have the same singular and plural forms	deer → deer
	sheep → sheep
	series → series

A. Spelling Plurals Correctly

Complete each sentence by writing the plural of the underlined word.

1. One <u>man</u> moved the chair, but it took several _____ to move the piano.

2. A single <u>deer</u> approached the apple tree, and then several more _____ appeared.

3. The sign is one <u>foot</u> from the sidewalk and six _____ from the tree.

4. In the flock of _____, only one <u>sheep</u> had horns.

5. This World <u>Series</u> is more exciting than all the other World _____ of the last ten years.

B. Writing Plural and Singular Forms

Match each description with a word from the list below. Then write the plural form of the word on the line.

        ox   woman   tooth   mouse   child

1. These are handy for chewing. _____

2. These usually pay a lower admission at the movies. _____

3. These are powerful beasts that pull plows. _____

4. All mothers and grandmothers are these. _____

5. Some people are as quiet as these. _____

Vocabulary and Spelling Strategies and Practice

Name .... Class .... Date ....

49 Troublesome Words I

Key Information

Below is a list of words that people often misspell. Circle those words you find difficult to spell.

absence	athlete	believe	canoe
accidentally	attendant	business	cemetery
adviser	beautiful	cafeteria	choir
answer	beginning	canceled	colonel

A. Spelling Words Correctly

Some of the words below are spelled correctly and some are not. If the spelling is correct, write *correct* on the line. If the spelling is incorrect, respell the word correctly.

1. caferteria _____
2. business _____
3. sematary _____
4. anser _____
5. absense _____

6. adviser _____
7. beginning _____
8. canceled _____
9. athelete _____
10. accidently _____

B. Proofreading

Circle the misspelled word or words in each sentence. Then spell them correctly on the line.

1. A cornel from the Civil War is buried in this cemetary. _____
2. Several students in the quier are also athletes. _____
3. The parking attendent accidentally left the keys in the car. _____
4. "Beleive me, begining was a challenge," said the business owner. _____
5. Roberta noticed an absense of bright plumage in many female birds. _____

Writer's Choice: Vocabulary and Spelling Strategies and Practice, Grade 6

Vocabulary and Spelling Strategies and Practice

Name .... Class .... Date ....

50 Troublesome Words II

Key Information

The words below are frequently misspelled. Are there words in this list that you have trouble spelling?

definite	February	government	humorous
descend	foreign	grammar	immediate
embarrass	funeral	guarantee	jewelry
environment	genius	height	laboratory

A. Spelling Words Correctly

Some of the words below are spelled correctly and some are not. If the spelling is correct, write *correct* on the line. If the spelling is incorrect, spell the word correctly.

1. grammar _____
2. definet _____
3. funeral _____
4. immediat _____
5. genius _____
6. enviornment _____
7. humorous _____
8. desend _____
9. February _____
10. height _____

B. Proofreading

Each sentence below contains one spelling error. Cross out the misspelled word, and spell it correctly on the line.

1. Her humorous jewlry included earrings that look like bananas. _____
2. The goverment plays a role in protecting the environment. _____
3. Hank was embarassed when he spilled alcohol in the laboratory. _____
4. Around here there is no guarantee of snow in Febuary. _____

Writer's Choice: Vocabulary and Spelling Strategies and Practice, Grade 6

Vocabulary and Spelling Strategies and Practice

Name .... Class .... Date ....

51 Troublesome Words III

Key Information

Here is a third list of words that are frequently misspelled. Notice that short words as well as long words can be difficult to spell.

library	muscle	ninety	permanent
license	necessary	occasion	physical
misspell	neighborhood	original	probably
molasses	niece	parallel	recognize

■ A. Spotting Spelling Errors

Circle the misspelled word in each pair from the list above. Then spell the word correctly on the line.

1. ninty, physical

2. necesary, niece

3. misspell, mussle

4. permanant, license

5. library, molassus

6. reconize, probably

7. lisense, library

8. necessary, mispell

9. origanal, neighborhood

10. parallel, occassion

■ B. Proofreading

Some sentences below contain a spelling error. Cross out the word that is spelled incorrectly, and spell it correctly on the line. If all the words are spelled correctly, write *correct*.

1. "The painting is probally an original," said the art dealer. _____

2. It is necessary to have a libary card if you want to check out a book. _____

3. The physical education teacher had us swing on the paralell bars. _____

4. Tom's nephew and niece live in his neighborhood. _____

5. Maggie recognized the new permanant custodian. _____

52 Troublesome Words IV

Key Information

Below is another list of words that are frequently misspelled. Circle the words that you have trouble spelling.

recommend	separate	technology	usually
restaurant	similar	theory	variety
rhythm	sincerely	traffic	various
schedule	succeed	truly	Wednesday

A. Spelling Words Correctly

Match each clue with a word from the list above. Write the missing letters in each word.

1. Between Tuesday and Thursday __ __ __ n __ __ __ __ __
2. To close a letter, write "Yours _____," __ __ __ __ y
3. You'll like the movie at the Rialto. I _____ it. _r_ __ __ o __ __ __ __ __
4. Alike but not identical __ __ __ __ __ __ a __
5. Most of the time but not always __ __ u __ __ __ y
6. Often provided by the drum section _r_ __ __ __ __ __
7. You pay to be served food here. __ __ __ t __ __ r __ __
8. The opposite of fail __ __ c __ __ __ __

B. Proofreading

Proofread each sentence to find a misspelled word. Spell the word correctly on the line.

1. The waiter at the restarant recommended the bird's nest soup. _____
2. Olivia and her sister have seperate bedrooms, but they have similar beds. _____
3. The bus did not arrive on skedule because of the traffic jam. _____
4. The researcher used the newest scientific tecnology to test her theory. _____
5. Alfredo plays a varety of instruments; his sense of rhythm is astounding. _____

52 Writer's Choice: Vocabulary and Spelling Strategies and Practice, Grade 6

Answers

PAGE 1
Pinkney Records a Round-the-World Voyage

Part A
1. recall
2. glimpse, visible
3. sprint, determination
4. navigation, latitude, longitude

Part B
Answers may be similar to the following.
1. dash, run swiftly
2. scientific method of determining position and course
3. see very briefly
4. able to be seen
5. degrees from 0 to 90 measuring distance from equator to pole

PAGE 2
Katz Rides the *Empire Builder*

Part A
Answers may be similar to the following.
1. lay down their guns, hold up their hands
2. keep firing, not give up ground
3. run for cover, leave the battlefield

Part B
1. The captain asked for additional troops in his telegram to the general.
2. The general decided to embellish his plain uniform with gold braid.
3. The manuscript gave an eyewitness account of the battle.
4. Evelyn had to resist the urge to get off the train and stay in the mountains.
5. The losing team would not retreat from its position in the debate.

PAGE 3
Boulanger Describes Nunataks

Part A
1. wildlife
2. resemble
3. isolated
4. variety
5. scamper
6. boulder
7. glacier
8. expand
9. continuously
10. vivid

Part B
Answers may be similar to the following.
1. Yes; a boulder's shape or color may resemble an egg's.
2. Yes; you might find a mountain goat, chipmunk, pika, marmot, or bird in an isolated area.
3. No; squirrels, dogs, or rabbits might scamper, but no variety of snake has feet to scamper on.

PAGE 4
Hamilton Narrates a Life

Part A
1. any two: significance, solemn, honor
2. any two: rally, organize, protest

Part B
1. influence
2. importance
3. greatly respect
4. gather, call together
5. well-informed
6. brave
7. disapproval, dissent
8. mass meeting

PAGE 5
Tribune Explores Hang Time

Part A
1. pose
2. explosive
3. chuckle
4. force
5. defy
6. gravity
7. challenge

Part B
Answers will include wording similar to the following.
1. the rules of a game, a leader who is unfair
2. sitting at a table with head resting on her hands, lying on the ground with the weight on one elbow
3. eyes, nose, forehead, chin
4. to drive a nail with a hammer, to lift lumber, to dig dirt with a shovel
5. an amusing story, a clever joke
6. an athletic event, a project for school, learning a skill

PAGE 6
Anderson Fights for the Planet

Part A
Answers may be similar to the following.
1. segment: one part of an insect's body
2. pollution: car exhaust
3. conserve: to take frequent rests when hiking so you have energy throughout the hike
4. convey: to cart bottles by car to a recycling center
5. persuade: to talk other students into signing a petition

Part B
Answers may be similar to the following.
1. To conserve energy, the boys walked at a comfortable pace and rested every mile.
2. Maleka checked the accuracy of the rainfall statistics in an atlas.

Answers

PAGE 7
***The Invisible Thread*, Yoshiko Uchida**

Part A
1. procedure, noun
2. immense, adjective
3. survey, verb
4. furiously, adverb
5. amble, verb
6. simultaneously, adverb

Part B
1. amble
2. immense
3. furiously
4. procedure
5. simultaneously
6. survey

PAGE 8
***Coast to Coast*, Betsy Byars**

Part A
1. hangar
2. altimeter
3. taxiway
4. idle
5. throttle
6. strut

Part B
Answers may be similar to the following.
1. The altimeter tells the pilot the altitude, or the airplane's height above the ground.
2. Yes, the airplane engine could run while the plane is in the hangar.
3. Without a strut the wing might vibrate, wobble, or even break off.
4. A runway is for landing and takeoff; a taxiway is for traveling between the runway and the terminal or other buildings.

PAGE 9
***Morning Girl*, Michael Dorris**

Part A
1. reflection
2. confessed
3. spiral
4. patience
5. complicated
6. memorized
7. curious

Part B
Answers may be similar to the following.
1. It had six parts and more than 100 questions.
2. It curved out from the flagpole in a winding circle.
3. He never looked at the book as he spoke.
4. He didn't get angry when they tracked mud all over the house.
5. She said she had taken two cookies without asking.
6. They took it to the library and found a book about trees.

PAGE 10
"The Jacket," Gary Soto

Part A
1. camouflage
2. braille
3. hurl
4. vinyl
5. vicious
6. profile
7. terrorist
8. embarrassed

Part B
Answers may be similar to the following.
1. The hunters wore camouflage so they would not be noticed as they stalked their prey in the woods.
2. The giant rock looked like the profile of Abraham Lincoln.
3. Marie moved her fingers over the words in braille.
4. Angelique hurled the tennis ball over the fence.
5. The dog became vicious because its owners did not treat it kindly.

PAGE 11
"Bathing Elephants," Peggy Thomson

Part A
1. fissure
2. wilt
3. infection
4. vibrate
5. unsightly
6. vulnerable
7. awe

Part B
Answers may be similar to the following.
1. Without his chest protector, the baseball catcher was vulnerable.
2. The bleachers began to vibrate from the stomping feet.
3. Yvonne wilted in disappointment when the winners were announced.
4. The O'Haras crossed the street to avoid the unsightly garbage.
5. Irvin had to maneuver gracefully to get through the crowded room.
6. Within three days all of the Patels had the infection.

PAGE 12
"Thanking the Birds," Joseph Bruchac

Part A
1. lecture
2. chickadee
3. ritual
4. anecdote
5. sacred
6. game
7. similarity
8. continent

Part B
1. cross out sacred; animals
2. cross out game; religion
3. cross out ritual; communication

Answers

PAGE 13
Context: Definition I

Part A
Answers may be similar to the following.
1. stationary: not moving; fixed in position
2. avid: enthusiastic
3. musty: smelling damp and moldy
4. voles: small mammals that dig tunnels in the ground
5. eluded: escaped

Part B
Answers may be similar to the following.
1. Both camels and sheep are ruminants, which means that they cough up partially digested food and chew it again.
2. As Tina told her story, she began to meander; in other words, she wandered or got off track.
3. For Anthony's family, celebrating grandmother's birthday was a tradition; that is, they got together year after year for a party.

PAGE 14
Context: Definition II

Part A
Answers may be similar to the following.
1. shrewd: clever
2. mineralogy: study of minerals
3. arroyos: dry creeks
4. burnished: polished
5. crevasse: deep, narrow crack

Part B
Answers may be similar to the following.
1. sharp spines
2. bright pink bird with a long curving neck and long legs
3. going for long walks in the woods or hills

PAGE 15
Context: Example I

Part A
Answers may be similar to the following.
1. transparent: clear, see-through
2. pampers: spoils
3. rodents: small mammals with sharp front teeth for gnawing
4. meager: skimpy; not enough
5. vague: not specific

Part B
Answers may be similar to the following.
1. Dressed for the ball, the young woman looked regal; for example, she wore a jeweled tiara and a richly embroidered dress.
2. The rooms of the old house were filled with antiques, such as a mahogany tea table made in 1776.

PAGE 16
Context: Example II

Part A
Answers may be similar to the following.
1. auburn: reddish brown
2. ungulates: animals with hooves
3. metropolis: very large city; large urban center
4. conifers: evergreen trees; trees with needles instead of broad leaves

Part B
Answers will vary.
1. live in coastal waters
2. an altimeter and an air-speed indicator
3. concrete walls, bare fields in winter

PAGE 17
Context: Comparison I

Part A
Answers should be similar to the following.
1. flexible, easy to mold
2. empty, without expression
3. fatal, deadly
4. agile, quick-footed

Part B
Answers may be similar to the following.
1. full of old papers and broken items
2. a flea's knee; a freckle
3. solemn, grave, harsh

PAGE 18
Context: Comparison II

Part A
1. likewise; ellipse: oval
2. also; somber: sad
3. likewise; restless: unable to be still
4. also; slither: slide on a slippery surface

Part B
Answers may be similar to the following.
1. Some baseball fans idolize Nolan Ryan; many also greatly admire Kirby Puckett.
2. Micki's apparel is always stylish; likewise, her sister's clothes are new and fashionable.

PAGE 19
Context: Contrast I

Part A
Answers may be similar to the following.
1. however; hostile: unfriendly
2. but; repels: drives away
3. but; severe: harsh, intense
4. however; fictional: not real, imaginary.

Writer's Choice: Vocabulary and Spelling Strategies and Practice, Grade 6

Answers

Part B

See the sentences in Part A for sample answers.

■ PAGE 20
Context: Contrast II

Part A

Answers may be similar to the following.
1. artificial: not natural; human-made
2. hindered: prevented; blocked

Part B

Answers may be similar to the following.
1. was a fake
2. get a chance to rest
3. very tidy
4. stared at the ground

■ PAGE 21
Word Parts: Roots I

Part A
1. scribe, description, manuscript, scribble, transcribe
2. dictate, contradict, dictionary

Part B
1. scribble
2. transcribe
3. dictate
4. manuscript
5. scribe

■ PAGE 22
Word Parts: Roots II

Part A
1. export; tell (carry back information)
2. infinite; vast, limitless
3. visible; clear to see
4. evident; plain, clear

Part B
1. infinite
2. export
3. final
4. define
5. porter
6. transportation
7. video
8. evidence

■ PAGE 23
Word Parts: Prefixes I

Part A
1. unripe
2. disable = to make incapable; unable = not able
3. undo
4. discontinue
5. unsophisticated
6. dishonest
7. unwilling
8. disapprove
9. dislike = to regard with disfavor; unlike = not alike
10. discourteous

Part B
1. dis-; not an advantage; drawback
2. un-; not grateful; without thanks
3. un-; undo a leash; let loose
4. dis-; lack of belief; rejection as untrue
5. dis-; undo a connection; separate

■ PAGE 24
Word Parts: Prefixes II

Part A
1. in-; not sincere; not genuine
2. non-; not fatal; not deadly
3. in-; not flexible; rigid
4. non-; without stopping; without ceasing
5. non-; not a resident; living elsewhere
6. in-; not moving; not in use; idle

Part B
1. nondairy product
2. inhospitable conditions
3. noncombatant
4. nonsense
5. involuntary reaction
6. nonmechanical toy

■ PAGE 25
Word Parts: Prefixes III

Part A
1. debug
2. pregame
3. defrost
4. dehydrate
5. prejudge

Part B
1. precolonial
2. descend
3. deprived
4. prerecorded

■ PAGE 26
Word Parts: Suffixes I

Part A
1. -er; a person who hires workers
2. -or; someone who collects
3. -or; a person who improves others' writing
4. -ist; a person who canoes
5. -or; someone who invents or devises
6. -ist; a person who is an expert in a science
7. -or; a person who watches
8. -or; a person who dictates; an absolute ruler
9. -or; someone who supervises or oversees
10. -er; someone who consumes something; a buyer of goods

Part B
1. governor, senator
2. manager, inventor
3. spectators, sailors, canoeists, skiers
4. editor, treasurer, collector
5. conductor, pianist

Answers

PAGE 27
Word Parts: Suffixes II

Part A
1. drink; safe to drink
   treat; can be treated or made safe
2. fashion; modern, trendy
   cred; hard to believe, amazing
3. convert; car with removable top
   think; unwise, not to be dared
4. favor; good, promising
   depend; reliable
5. sense; rational, reasonable
   vis; in open view

Part B
1. digestible
2. sensible
3. readable
4. believable
5. convertible

PAGE 28
Word Parts: Suffixes III

Part A
1. still + -ness; state of being still; calm
2. humor + -less; without humor
3. wire + -less; without wires
4. gentle + -ness; quality of being gentle; mildness
5. penny + -less; without money; broke

Part B
1. Yes—if it runs on batteries
2. No—all runners eventually slow down or become tired
3. Yes—if the person doesn't laugh or make jokes
4. Yes—if it was unsuccessful

PAGE 29
Synonyms I

Part A
Answers may be similar to the following.
1. automobile, vehicle
2. avid, enthusiastic
3. consider, contemplate
4. sturdy, long-lasting
5. soar, slide

Part B
Answers may be similar to the following.
1. red
2. confused
3. stormy
4. scolded
5. troubled

PAGE 30
Synonyms II

Part A
1. awkward
2. severe
3. leery
4. pliable
5. lucid
6. grueling
7. surly
8. sufficient
9. incorrect
10. tranquil

Part B
1. amble, stroll, saunter
2. babble, jabber, chatter
3. shimmer, glitter, glimmer

PAGE 31
Antonyms I

Part A
1. silly
2. severe
3. artificial
4. taciturn
5. energetic
6. ruddy
7. prompt
8. courteous
9. authentic
10. sweltering

Part B
1. sweltering, frigid
2. solemn, silly
3. authentic, fake
4. taciturn, talkative
5. prompt, tardy

PAGE 32
Antonyms II

Part A
1. disadvantage
2. nonconformist
3. unexceptional
4. unembarrassed
5. nonallergic
6. disbelief, nonbelief, or unbelief
7. discourteous
8. ungrammatical or nongrammatical
9. inexact
10. infirm

Part B
Examples may be similar to the following.
1. unmusical; The car made an unmusical sound when it hit the curb.
2. incomplete; After he lost a rook, Chris had an incomplete set of chess pieces.
3. nontechnical; Shanna used a nontechnical word instead of scientific jargon.

PAGE 33
Homonyms

Part A
1. over their heads
2. when you're finished
3. their own house
4. its own batteries
5. your first visit

Answers

Part B
1. too
2. principal
3. here
4. principle
5. two

PAGE 34
Borrowed Words

Part A
1. Hindi
2. Old English
3. Arabic
4. West African
5. German
6. Taino
7. Latin
8. Greek (ancient)
9. Old Norse
10. Irish

Part B
1. parent
2. moccasin
3. café
4. honcho
5. blitz

PAGE 35
Using a Dictionary I

Part A
Possible meanings include the following.
1. (noun) large basket with a lid for carrying or storing food or laundry; (verb) to restrict the movement of; interfere with
2. (verb) (1) to make short, rapid, sharp sounds; (2) to chatter or utter rapidly; (3) to move with a clatter; (4) to upset or unnerve; (noun) (1) sharp clattering sound; (2) device that makes a rattle

Part B
Answers may be similar to the following.
1. The speaker bored his audience because he spoke in a monotone.
2. Some farmers and ranchers keep their animals in a pen.
3. The interviewer screened the applicants to make sure each had a diploma.
4. The box's contents were dusty and jumbled.

PAGE 36
Using a Dictionary II

Part A
1. convex
2. dubious
3. quirky
4. ridicule
5. rhythm
6. aviation

Part B
1. It is pronounced.
2. It sounds like the *i* in *pit*.
3. It begins with the same sound as *church*.
4. Yes, it does.
5. No, they do not rhyme.
6. Yes, they are pronounced the same.

PAGE 37
Using a Dictionary III

Part A
1. excavation
2. cave
3. pastime
4. training
5. plentiful

Part B
Answers may be similar to the following.
1. betray, dupe
2. trip, slip
3. fracture, splinter
4. exhausted, sleepy
5. tranquil, serene

PAGE 38
Using a Dictionary IV

Part A
1. garter
2. garnish
3. garter snake
4. garrison
5. garnishing

Part B
1. garnish
2. They are not dangerous, because they are non-poisonous.
3. It is pronounced like the first syllable of *garnish*.
4. garnish, garrison, garter
5. It means "the bend of the knee."

PAGE 39
Using a Dictionary V

Part A
1. a person who has control over something
2. highly skilled
3. become expert in
4. person of great skill or ability
5. most important

Part B
Answers may be similar to the following.
1. Latin
2. Josh worked all weekend to master his juggling routine.
3. Katrina found the master key in the drawer.
4. In the show, Rosa played the pupil and Marcus played the master.

Answers

PAGE 40
Using a Dictionary VI

Part A
1. gaggle
2. swarm
3. pride
4. bevy
5. litter

Part B
1. It borrowed the word from Dutch.
2. drom-e-dar-y
3. triumph; overcome
4. It is a verb.
5. It is pronounced like *sh*; other examples include *creation* and *nation*.
6. It rhymes with *daze*.

PAGE 41
Spelling Rules: *ie* and *ei*

Part A
1. leisure
2. grieve
3. species
4. freight
5. weird

Part B
Sentences should contain one or more of the following words or others that follow the pattern.
1. receive, ceiling, receipt
2. chief, believe, grief
3. freight, eight, veil, neighbor
4. weird, either, neither, height

PAGE 42
Spelling Rules: Suffixes and the Silent *e*

Part A
1. famous
2. careful
3. shiny
4. hoeing
5. finest
6. manageable
7. outrageous
8. dodging

Part B
1. faking
2. excitable
3. tasty
4. changeable
5. agreeing
6. peaceable
7. completely
8. judging

PAGE 43
Spelling Rules: Suffixes and the Final *y*

Part A
1. tried
2. payable
3. fluffier
4. enjoyed
5. readying

Part B
1. copying
2. fuzzier
3. tarried
4. hurrying
5. holiness

PAGE 44
Spelling Rules: Doubling the Final Consonant

Part A
1. preference
2. submitted
3. snacking
4. forgetful
5. planned

Part B
1. whipped
2. training
3. regretted
4. offered
5. drifting

PAGE 45
Spelling Rules: Forming Compound Words

Part A
1. kickoff
2. kickstand
3. homespun
4. skywrite
5. fairground
6. seafarer
7. skyscraper
8. eyedropper

Part B
Answers may be similar to the following.
1. mobile; Dennis checks out books whenever the book-mobile comes to his neighborhood.
2. cake; The fruitcake was full of nuts, dried cherries, raisins, and orange peel.
3. air; Andrea sent the package to France by airmail.
4. skate; Nick always wears kneepads and a helmet when he rides his skateboard.

PAGE 46
Spelling Rules: General Rules for Forming Plurals

Part A
1. journeys
2. rodeos
3. crosses
4. elves
5. swatches
6. solos
7. dishes
8. dairies
9. tiffs
10. faxes

Writer's Choice: Vocabulary and Spelling Strategies and Practice, Grade 6

Answers

Part B
1. heroes
2. ways
3. halves
4. churches

PAGE 47
Spelling Rules: Special Rules for Forming Plurals I

Part A
1. Gomezes
2. textbooks
3. vice-presidents
4. brothers-in-law
5. Marches

Part B
1. editors-in-chief
2. iceboxes
3. runners-up
4. sweatshirts
5. lifeguards

PAGE 48
Spelling Rules: Special Rules for Forming Plurals II

Part A
1. men
2. deer
3. feet
4. sheep
5. Series

Part B
1. tooth, teeth
2. child, children
3. ox, oxen
4. woman, women
5. mouse, mice

PAGE 49
Troublesome Words I

Part A
1. cafeteria
2. correct
3. cemetery
4. answer
5. absence
6. correct
7. correct
8. correct
9. athlete
10. accidentally

Part B
1. colonel; cemetery
2. choir
3. attendant
4. Believe; beginning
5. absence

PAGE 50
Troublesome Words II

Part A
1. correct
2. definite
3. correct
4. immediate
5. correct
6. environment
7. humorous
8. descend
9. correct
10. correct

Part B
1. jewelry
2. government
3. embarrassed
4. February

PAGE 51
Troublesome Words III

Part A
1. ninety
2. necessary
3. muscle
4. permanent
5. molasses
6. recognize
7. license
8. misspell
9. original
10. occasion

Part B
1. probably
2. library
3. parallel
4. correct
5. permanent

PAGE 52
Troublesome Words IV

Part A
1. Wednesday
2. truly
3. recommend
4. similar
5. usually
6. rhythm
7. restaurant
8. succeed

Part B
1. restaurant
2. separate
3. schedule
4. technology
5. variety